Prayers That Avail Much

Volume 1

The Effectual Fervent Prayer
Of a Righteous Man Availeth Much

Harrison House, Inc
Tulsa, Oklahoma

Prayers That Avail Much, Volume 1, Portable Gift Book
ISBN 0-89274-960-1
Copyright © 1995 by
Harrison House, Inc.
P. O. Box 35035
Tulsa, OK 74153

Published by HARRISON HOUSE, INC.
P. O. Box 35035
Tulsa, OK 74153

Introduction

"The earnest (heartfelt, continued) prayer of a righteous man makes tremendous power available [dynamic in its working]."

James 5:16 AMP

Prayer is fellowshipping with the Father – a vital, personal contact with God Who is more than enough and wants to meet your daily needs.

Prayer is not to be a meaningless religious ritual with no power. It is to be effective and accurate and bring *results*.

God watches over His Word to perform it. (Jer. 1:12.) That is why we designed this special edition of *Prayers That Avail Much* – to give you the opportunity to pray God's Word and watch Him fulfill His promises.

Based upon the bestselling original book, *Prayers That Avail Much, Volume 1*, this compact, easy-to-use edition offers a scriptural prayer and a faith-filled confession to help you speak the Word. As you pray these scriptural prayers, your faith will grow and your heart will be encouraged.

Prayers That Avail Much, Volume 1, Portable Gift Book – praying with the power of God's Word!

Thank You, Lord Jesus, for baptizing me with the Holy Ghost and fire – fire to run the course You've set before me with accuracy, precision and victory! I am being filled with You day by day, Holy Spirit. Your presence is a consuming fire in my bones! Your fire is burning out of me everything unlike You, in Jesus' name. Amen.

Luke 3:16

———————— C O N F E S S I O N ————————

I will stay pure by reading God's Word
and following its rules. (Ps. 119:9.)

Heavenly Father, thank You for Your covenant promises for the tither – the person who gives of the firstfruits (the tenth) of all their income. You said for the person who brings their tithe to the local storehouse (the local church) where they are fed, You will open the windows of heaven upon them. You will pour out blessings there is not room enough to receive. You will rebuke the devourer, and all nations will call the tither blessed! In other words, the world will see the prosperity of those who tithe. Father, I want to give You praise and thanksgiving because of Your goodness to me, in Jesus' name. Amen.

Malachi 3:8-12

CONFESSION

My tithe belongs to God. My offerings – whether of finances, time, or talent – also belong to Him!

Father, You are the One Who builds relationships and friendships. My dearest Friend is You, Lord Jesus. Because my relationship with You is intact, it is easier to interact with others and build good relationships with them. Thank You for the friends You have brought into my life, Lord. We speak into each other's lives to uplift and encourage. We laugh and cry together. We correct one another. We trust each other. We are loyal to one another. Thank You for enriching my life with special friends, in Jesus' name. Amen.

Proverbs 17:17; Proverbs 18:24; John 15:13,14

──────── CONFESSION ────────

My greatest Friend is Jesus Christ, Who laid down
His life that I might live! (John 15:13.)

Heavenly Father, thank You that the original foundation of education in our land was based upon the Bible. Textbooks were infiltrated with Your Word. You said we could decree a thing and it would be established. Father, in Jesus' name, I decree that the educational system return to its roots, in both public and private Christian schools. Thank You that teachers in both public and private schools are filled with Your wisdom. I decree a revival in our land in the educational system, Lord. May You be magnified in teaching that revolves around the whole person – the spirit as well as the body and the mind. Hallelujah!

Job 22:28; Psalm 11:3

───────────────── C O N F E S S I O N ─────────────────

My children have the mind of Christ. (1 Cor. 2:16.)

Father, in Your Son Jesus Christ I have refuge (safety, peace and protection) from the storms of life because He is my Refuge. In Him I have wisdom and authority to overcome every work of the enemy because He is Wisdom and Authority. In Him I have provision for every need because He is Provision. In Him I possess an abundant spiritual inheritance of salvation, deliverance, healing and life forevermore because He is the Resurrection and the Life!

John 11:25; 2 Peter 1:3,4

—————————— CONFESSION ——————————

I live and move and have my being in Jesus Christ! (Acts 17:28.)

Lord Jesus, You said to Jairus regarding his daughter who had physically died, "Don't be afraid; just believe, and she will be healed." Believing in You will take me beyond the realm of impossibility. It will take me beyond man's limited rationale. As I believe You and Your Word, Father, You will cause many situations coined "impossible" to become realities, in Jesus' name. Amen.

Mark 9:23,24; Luke 8:50

——————————— CONFESSION ———————————

I will be courageous, for God will do exactly
what He said He would do. (Acts 27:25.)

Lord Jesus, You said that whatever is hidden will be disclosed. Whatever is concealed will be brought out into the open. Plots of wickedness cannot prevail against me. Man's carnal, alternative, or less-than-excellent agendas cannot prevail in my life. Your will and Your truth reign in my life, Lord! I am in a championship race. In the name of Jesus, I will run it well! Amen.

Mark 4:22; Luke 8:17

CONFESSION

I will run with patience, persistence and excellence the race that God has set before me. (Heb. 12:1.)

 Father, because Jesus resides in me through the Holy Spirit, I am the salt and light of Your Kingdom in the earth. I season others with Your light, and with Your love. And I give off a sweet fragrance of the knowledge of You, Lord Jesus. Thank You, Father, for leading me in triumph in every situation I face in Jesus' name. Amen.

Matthew 5:13-16; 2 Corinthians 2:14

———— C O N F E S S I O N ————

The fragrance of the knowledge of Jesus Christ
flows through me to others. (2 Cor. 2:14.)

Heavenly Father, teach me to delegate authority when it would be profitable in Your sight to do so, just as Jethro taught Moses. Help me to be sensitive to Your still, small voice, Lord, so I will not wear myself out with needless activities. Instead, my time and talents will be maximized for the good of the entire Body of Christ, in Jesus' name. Amen.

Exodus 18:13-26; 1 Kings 19:12

CONFESSION

*I am imitating the management principles
and procedures that were successful in God's Word!*

Father, I have committed myself to spend quality time in prayer and in fellowship with You each day. You said in Your Word to call unto You and You will show me great and unsearchable things. You will reveal divine secrets to me which I know nothing about. These secrets are keys for putting me in a top-ranking position for the benefit of Your Kingdom, in Jesus' name. Thank You, Lord, for the trust You have placed in me to be a good steward of Your secrets. Amen.

Jeremiah 33:3

─────────── C O N F E S S I O N ───────────

The unsearchable riches of Christ are loosed unto me that
I might be a greater blessing for God's Kingdom in the earth.

Father God, Peter spoke to the beggar at the temple gate called Beautiful, crippled from birth, "Silver or gold I do not have, but what I have I give you." Peter shared Your healing virtue, Lord Jesus. The man rose up and walked,  absolutely whole! Lord, I will share with others what You have given me. With Your resurrection life, I will heal, deliver and lift others from where they are to where You want them to be, in Jesus' name. Amen.

Acts 3:1-12,16

—————— CONFESSION ——————

Jesus Christ of Nazareth will lift me up,
encourage me and help me. (James 4:10, TLB.)

Father, wisdom and knowledge of You are the stabilizing forces of my life. I will not be destroyed for lack of knowledge, because I daily fill my mind and heart with Your Word. A spirit of wisdom and revelation dominates me, Lord, enabling me to gain even greater insight into the secret workings of Your Kingdom.

Isaiah 33:6; Hosea 4:6; Ephesians 1:17, AMP

─────── CONFESSION ───────

The Holy Spirit gives me a revelation of God's Word,
which provides supernatural wisdom to overcome
natural obstacles and negative circumstances!

Father, in Jesus' name, I am storing up treasures in heaven. Moth and rust can't touch these riches. Thieves can't break in and steal them. They cannot be corrupted. The treasures I am storing up include financial support to further Your work upon the earth, Lord Jesus. It includes prayer for the heathen as well as for the saints. It includes time given to encourage and lift someone else with Your Word. It includes feeding and clothing the poor. Because my heart is focused upon heavenly treasures, Father, Your blessings crown my life, in Jesus' name. Amen.

Matthew 6:19-21

———————————— C O N F E S S I O N ————————————

The Lord delights in my well-being. (Ps. 35:27.)

Father, You said that as Your children, we are to guard and keep the harmony and oneness produced by Your Spirit. Thank You for the harmony in my marriage, Lord Jesus, which causes my home to be a haven of peace. Open communication takes the place of strife. Thank You for the tenderness that is expressed, which promotes love and kindness. Thank You for the unity we share. Greed and selfish pursuits have no place in our marriage relationship. In the name of Jesus, our focus is on the welfare of one another. Amen.

Ephesians 4:3; 1 Peter 3:11, AMP

———————— CONFESSION ————————

Because we are of one mind and we live in peace and
harmony with each other, God's peace and love dominate
my marriage, home and family! (2 Cor. 13:11.)

By an act of my will, I have allowed my flesh to be crucified with You, Lord Jesus. The real life I now have within my spirit, body and mind is the result of trusting in You. Thank You for seeing eternal value in me, Lord. Through the work of the Holy Spirit, my value is escalating daily! Glory to God!

Galatians 2:20

———————— CONFESSION ————————

God has placed a crown of glory and
honor upon my head. (Ps. 8:5, TLB.)

Heavenly Father, my life is a testimony to the fact that Your glory fills the earth. No one will be able to say they didn't know of You. I, along with each believer, will live in such a way that You are revealed. In Character! Integrity! Faithfulness! Love! Joy! Peace! Regardless of circumstances! In control regardless of life's storms that may be raging! In complete victory in every aspect of this life, in Jesus' name. Amen.

Numbers 14:21; Habakkuk 2:14

——————————— CONFESSION ———————————

I will share the testimony of what the Lord has done for me so no one can say they never knew the Lord. (Jer. 31:34, AMP.)

Father, You are gracious and compassionate. You are slow to anger and abounding in love toward me. Though I am walking with You, I am turning to You with a fresh zeal today. As I seek You in fasting and prayer, I want to be even more fine-tuned to Your Spirit than ever before. Cleanse me, Lord, of any attitude that would hinder my walk with You. Remove from me inverted vision that would cause me to keep my eyes on my own concerns and interests rather than on You and on the needs of others, in Jesus' name. Amen.

Joel 2:12,13

——————————— C O N F E S S I O N ———————————

The Holy Spirit keeps and guides me in God's love. (Jude 21.)

21

Father God, I desire the rich, eternal treasures of Your kingdom, where Jesus Christ is seated at Your right hand. Nothing can compare with Your riches, Father. In them are life, health, healing, soundness, deliverance, and provision. In them are strategies that will disarm the tricks of the devil. In them are restoration and reconciliation. In Your treasures are the keys for stopping Satan's destruction of life – whether it be of the abortion of babies or the abortion of Your visions and dreams, Lord. Your treasures are life-giving! Amen.

Colossians 3:1-3

——————————— C O N F E S S I O N ———————————

The treasures of sound and godly
wisdom are mine. (Prov. 2:7, AMP.)

Father, as a citizen of Your kingdom, I am living a life that is pleasing to You. I am standing firm with the standards of Your Word as my guide. I am united with You in Spirit and in purpose. I am single-mindedly contending for the faith. I am pursuing the destiny which You hand-crafted just for me, Father! Every day is one of great accomplishments for Your Kingdom, in Jesus' name. Amen.

Philippians 1:27, AMP

──────────── C O N F E S S I O N ────────────

I have the same attitude, purpose and humble mind
as Jesus Christ. He is my example for greatness! (Phil. 2:5.)

Father God, with the enablement of the Holy Spirit, I can run through any troop. With the Holy Spirit's help, I can leap over any wall. It might be a wall of adversity. Symptoms of a serious illness. Heartbreak. A broken relationship. Lack. You will lift me over every hurdle! I refuse to be denied of that which You have provided for me, Father, in Jesus' name. Amen.

2 Samuel 22:30

CONFESSION

With God nothing is impossible to me! (Matt. 19:26.)

Father God, I desire to be a repairer of the breach — one who brings healing to the brokenhearted and strengthens the unity of the Body of Christ. You said in Your Word that two cannot walk together in harmony unless they be in agreement. You also said if two will agree on earth as touching anything, it shall be done for them. I agree with my brothers and sisters in the Body of Christ that this is the hour for the wealth of the wicked to come into the hands of the righteous, that Your assignments will be completed and the alarm will be sounded of Your soon return, Lord Jesus!

Psalm 133; Proverbs 13:22; Isaiah 58:12; Amos 3:3; Matthew 18:19,20

——————————— C O N F E S S I O N ———————————

I am earnestly striving to keep the harmony and oneness
in the body of Christ, produced by the Holy Spirit.

Lord Jesus, You are the resurrection and the life. Your resurrection power is alive in me. I am appointed and anointed by You to abound in eternal work for Your Kingdom. My victory is assured, because I walk uprightly in You. Your resurrection power in me raises havoc with the plans of the devil! I'm not just existing, but I am accomplishing great exploits for Your Kingdom. The best is yet to come, in Jesus' name! Amen.

John 11:25; 1 Corinthians 15:58, TLB

———————————— C O N F E S S I O N ————————————

No good thing will God withhold from me! (Ps. 84:11.)

Heavenly Father, You said in Your Word that the worker is worthy of his wages. Help me to be one of the finest workers any employer has ever seen. Diligent! Accurate! Dependable! Always on time! Respectful of company rules! Cooperative! Friendly! Let me represent You well, Lord Jesus, and help me to remember that I am not limited by a paycheck. Unlimited heavenly prosperity is available to me now for the work of Your Kingdom in the earth, in Jesus' name. Amen.

1 Timothy 5:18

——————————— CONFESSION ———————————

I am diligent with the time and talents God has invested in me!

Holy Spirit, because You have helped me to adjust my priorities and my focus to seek first the Kingdom of God and His righteousness, everything I need is provided each day — from divine understanding, connections, wisdom, promotion, health, riches and honor.

Matthew 6:33

———————— C O N F E S S I O N ————————

Because the Lord is my Shepherd,
I have everything I need! (Ps. 23:1, TLB.)

28

Heavenly Father, because of Your compassion and faithfulness, You have established, strengthened and kept me from the evil one. Your Word guards me from satanic attacks. I am strong in You, Lord, and in Your mighty power.  I am dressed in the armor You have provided for me, which repels the attacks of the devil. The good fight of faith — believing and speaking Your Word — puts me over in the daily affairs of this life. There's no room for defeat in me! Hallelujah!

Ephesians 6:10-18; 2 Thessalonians 3:3

──────────── CONFESSION ────────────

The power in God's right hand shatters
the enemy's works in my life! (Ex. 15:6.)

Heavenly Father, because of Jesus' completed work at Calvary, I have been given boldness for timidity. Faith for fear. Confidence for inferiority. Strength for weakness. Prosperity for lack. Acceptance for condemnation. Security for insecurity. Stability for instability. Soundness of mind for emotional instability. Love for hate. Peace for strife. In You, Lord Jesus, I am a new creature with positive attributes!

Psalm 34:4; Romans 8:1; 2 Corinthians 5:17; 2 Timothy 1:7

——————————— C O N F E S S I O N ———————————

My roots go down deep in the soil of God's love. (Eph. 3:17 TLB.)

Heavenly Father, Your peace drives out the fear and torment of the enemy and keeps me calm. Your peace settles my questions. It guards my heart and mind. It soothes my spirit. It causes me to be stable in the midst of the storms of life. It is more important to me, Lord, to be a peacemaker than to be right in a controversy! In the name of Jesus, Your peace and wisdom dominate my human spirit. Amen.

John 14:27; John 16:33, AMP; 2 Corinthians 13:11;

Galatians 5:22; Philippians 4:7; Colossians 3:15

———————————— CONFESSION ————————————

Nothing will offend me or make me stumble, because
God's peace rules and reigns in my life. (Ps. 119:165, AMP.)

Father, thank You for causing my thoughts to come in line with Your Word and Your will for my life, which are one and the same. Purify my thoughts and motives so they are acceptable in Your sight. As I roll my works upon You, Father, the plans You have for me will be established and they will succeed. I will no longer be hindered by human thoughts about my performance, but I will be encouraged to run even faster with Your vision because Your hand is upon me, Lord. Hallelujah!

Proverbs 16:1-3, AMP

——————— C O N F E S S I O N ———————

My steps are ordered by the Lord. (Ps. 37:23.)

Father, because of Jesus' victory over the devil at Calvary, divine favor is available to me — favor in my relationships, career, ministry, marriage and family. Because I am clothed with Your favor, Lord, You cause me to ride upon the high places of the earth.

Psalm 5:12; Isaiah 58:14

———— C O N F E S S I O N ————

The favor of the Lord surrounds me as a shield.

Father, because Your Spirit is alive in me, I am swift to hear, and I am a good listener. I am slow to speak, and I choose my words with grace. I am slow to become angry. Anger, exasperation, fury and indignation give an open door to the enemy if not resolved quickly. These negative traits of the devil have no place in me. Before the sun goes down each day, help me to examine my own heart to make sure I am filled only with Your positive traits, in Jesus' precious name. Amen.

Ephesians 4:26,27 AMP; James 1:19,20

───────────── C O N F E S S I O N ─────────────

My spirit, dominated by the Holy Spirit, bears His fruit of love,
joy, peace, longsuffering, gentleness, goodness, faith,
meekness and temperance. (Gal. 5:22,23.)

Lord Jesus, You became a curse for me. You redeemed me to make me an heir of Abraham's blessings. I receive Your inheritance of abundance for lack; healing, wholeness and soundness for sickness and disease; divine wisdom for man's foolishness; life for death; victory for defeat; and knowledge of You for ignorance, Lord. In the name of Jesus, I will be all You have destined me to be! Hallelujah!

Galatians 3:13,14

───────────── C O N F E S S I O N ─────────────

God is working His plan in my life, which causes me to prosper, to be protected and to have hope and a terrific future! (Jer. 29:11.)

Father, there isn't a challenge I will ever face that will be too hard for You to solve. Nothing can outsmart You. The world's wisdom is foolishness in Your sight. Your wisdom is increasing in me through meditation of Your Word. It leads, guides and protects me. It gives me greater insight and credentials than the world has to offer. You have said in Your Word that the person who gets wisdom loves his own soul. He who cherishes understanding will prosper. Hallelujah!

Jeremiah 32:27; 1 Corinthians 3:19

———————— C O N F E S S I O N ————————

I am daily increasing in godly wisdom,
knowledge and understanding.

Father, I accept and yield myself completely to Your tailor-made plans for my life. I will go where You want me to go and do what You want me to do. I can do all things through You, Lord Jesus, because You are my strength and enablement through the Holy Spirit.

Acts 1:8; Philippians 4:13

———————————— CONFESSION ————————————

Because I am willing and obedient to the Lord,
I am eating the good of the land! (Isa. 1:19.)

Heavenly Father, everything I will ever need for life and godliness is found in the application of the knowledge of You. I will meditate continually in Your Word to better understand the inheritance You have given to me. Then I will personalize Your promises for my life to the point that I will rule and reign as a king and a priest in this earth. Nothing of man or of the enemy will be able to overrule the Spirit in which I live and move and have my being. Amen.

2 Peter 1:3; Revelation 1:6

CONFESSION

Through studying the Word and allowing it to work in my heart, I will know the Lord more intimately each day!

Father, thank You for flooding me with creative ideas – ideas that will influence kings, conquer kingdoms, administer justice, shut the mouths of lions and change sinners to saints. You are Creativity, Lord, and because I am anchored into all that You are, I will be like You!

Proverbs 8:12; Hebrews 11:33,34

——————— CONFESSION ———————

I am being transformed daily into the image and likeness of God!

Father, You are a revealer of mysteries and secrets. My spirit is fine-tuned to Your Spirit so I'll not miss anything You are trying to impart to me. My body is under the dominion of Your Spirit. I have renewed my mind with Your Word. I feed my spirit consistently on the divine diet of Your Word, which is life and health to me. In Jesus' name, I am pleasing to You, Father, because of my hunger to know You and love You more. Amen.

Proverbs 4:20-22; Daniel 2:28,47

C O N F E S S I O N

*I have life and peace because my mind
is controlled by the Holy Spirit. (Rom. 8:6.)*

Heavenly Father, You have blessed the work of my hands. Because You love, accept and approve of me, I will be strong even when my flesh feels weak. I will not give up when natural circumstances indicate that I'm down for the count and almost out. I will stand firm until Your will prevails and Satan's plans have been fully demolished. I'll not be moved until I hear You say, "Well done, good and faithful servant."

Deuteronomy 28:12; 2 Chronicles 15:7; 1 Corinthians 15:58

———————————— C O N F E S S I O N ————————————

I am destined to be the winner in every skirmish with the devil.

Father God, I will obey the command of Your Word to not be unequally yoked together in any relationship. Righteousness and wickedness have nothing in common. Neither do believers and unbelievers...light and darkness...the temple of God and idols...cleanness and uncleanness. Because my body is Your temple, Lord, and I have been separated unto You, I will maintain the standard of purity You have established for my life, in Jesus' name. Amen.

2 Corinthians 6:14-18

CONFESSION

Because bad company corrupts good character,
I will be careful to be hooked up with people
of like spirit. (1 Cor. 15:33.)

Father, You have chosen me, like Abraham, to be a carrier of Your life and blessings to others, keeping Your ways and doing what is right and just in Your sight. I will partake of solid spiritual food daily so I am able to distinguish good from evil and teach others of Your righteousness, in Jesus' name. Amen.

Genesis 22:17,18

——————————— CONFESSION ———————————

I will live a life worthy of the calling
I have received from the Lord. (Eph. 4:1.)

Father, You alone are God! I bow my knees unto You and unto Your Son Jesus Christ. I'll not bow to other gods and worship them. You have set before me life and death, blessing and cursing. I choose life this very day that both my seed and I may truly live! Father, You are my life and the length of my days. I will dwell in the land You have given me, and I will excel for You in it, in Jesus' name. Amen.

Deuteronomy 30:19,20

CONFESSION

Long life, health and prosperity are mine
as I walk in obedience to the Lord!

Father, You said in Your Word through Paul, "Where the Spirit of the Lord is, there is liberty — emancipation from bondage, freedom." Because of the Holy Spirit's abiding presence in my life, I live in freedom. I will not be hampered or ensnared again with the yoke of slavery from which You have set me free, in the name of Jesus. Amen.

2 Corinthians 3:17; Galatians 5:1, AMP

————————— C O N F E S S I O N —————————

Because the Son has made me free,
I am unquestionably free! (John 8:36, AMP.)

Heavenly Father, because I am in covenant with You, all of the promises of Your Word belong to me. All of my children are taught of You, Lord. They are obedient to You. Your peace dominates them in their spirit, body and mind. Because of their great love for You, Lord Jesus, they are sharing You with their friends and teachers. Their communication with You and with others is open and Spirit led. In Jesus' name, they are being transformed into champions for God's Kingdom! Hallelujah!

Isaiah 54:13

—————————— CONFESSION ——————————

Just as God framed the world with His Word,
I am framing my children with His Word! (Heb. 11:3.)

Thank You, Father, for the keys of Your Kingdom which You have freely given me to exercise Your power and authority in the earth. I will overcome every challenge I face because of exercising the authority You have invested in me through Your name, Your blood, Your Word and Your Spirit. I will also use this authority to liberate others as I stand in the gap on their behalf in Jesus' name.

Matthew 16:19; Luke 10:19; Matthew 16:19

———————————— CONFESSION ————————————

I am more than a conqueror through Christ Jesus
Who loves me! (Rom. 8:37.)

Father, I am living by every Word that has come out of Your mouth. My spiritual diet is just as important as my physical diet. While natural food energizes my physical body, Your Word energizes my spirit man. With Your help, Holy Spirit, I will maintain a proper balance in both diets so I can maximize the potential divinely deposited within me in Jesus' name. Amen.

Deuteronomy 8:3; Matthew 4:4

——————— C O N F E S S I O N ———————

*Jesus Christ, the Bread of Life, orchestrates my
natural and spiritual diets! (John 6:35.)*

My words are as Your Words, Lord — as silver tried in a furnace, purified seven times — they are filled with wisdom and they chart the course of my destiny and the destiny of others. They create life rather than death, blessing rather than cursing, peace rather than strife, harmony rather than disharmony, abundance rather than lack, and healing rather than disease.

Psalm 12:6

―――――――― C O N F E S S I O N ――――――――

The life of God flows from my tongue, creating an atmosphere of His presence everywhere I go! (Prov. 18:21.)

Heavenly Father, I am not limited in doing what You have asked me to do, because Your Word says, "Everything is possible for him who believes." The setting, the finances, the connections, the people and the anointing needed to fulfill Your call upon my life have already been provided in Jesus' name. I am calling those things which are not as though they already were, because You have made every provision I will ever need, Lord! Thank You!

Mark 9:23; Romans 4:17

——————————— CONFESSION ———————————

*No word from God is without power
or impossible of fulfillment. (Luke 1:37, AMP.)*

Father God, thank You for giving my boss Your wisdom and ability. Thank You for flooding his/her heart with Your anointing to complete the tasks You have set before him/her. Lord Jesus, be my boss's pacesetter. Help him/her to turn the opportunities for stress into productivity. Help him/her to turn challenges into stepping stones to further growth. I ask that You shower my boss with Your approval today, Lord Jesus. Cause him/her to find favor with his/her superiors. Bless and protect him/her, in Jesus' name. Amen.

Luke 2:52; 1 Timothy 2:1-3

─────────────── C O N F E S S I O N ───────────────

I will work for my boss as if I am working for Christ —
with diligence, dependability, accuracy, kindness and respect.

Father God, You said in Your Word that Stephen was a man full of Your grace and power. He performed many signs and wonders among the people. I lay my total life down to You. I yield to Your plans for my life. I will anchor myself into Your Word as never before. It will be said of me, like Stephen, that no one could resist the wisdom or the Spirit by Whom I spoke! Hallelujah!

Acts 6:8-10

——————————— C O N F E S S I O N ———————————

God's wisdom and understanding are mine.
They are better than gold or silver! (Prov. 16:16.)

Father, to believe You and Your Word, even in the midst of the storms of life, provides a place of rest for me. In the midst of seemingly impossible demands, deadlines and tasks at hand, my heart and mind can be at rest in You. Strength and boldness are released into me as I confidently rest upon Your promises, Father. In Your presence, I am refreshed, restored and renewed in Jesus' name. Amen.

Isaiah 30:15; Mark 6:31; Hebrews 4:1-4,10,11

—————————— CONFESSION ——————————

The rest of the Lord, which I have entered,
yields the fruit of joy, strength and refreshing.

Heavenly Father, I will plant love, finances, the Word of truth and life, kindness and blessings in the lives of others in the midst of famine. I will reap a hundred-fold of like kind in the same year, just as Isaac did. Seedtime and harvest are as much a part of the functioning of Your Kingdom, Lord, as are summer and winter, day and night, and cold and heat. Though instability may reign in the economy around me, in Jesus' name I will prosper because of obedience to the principles of Your Word, Father.

Genesis 8:22; Genesis 26

CONFESSION

The windows of heaven are open upon my life,
and God's blessings are overtaking me! (Mal. 3:10.)

Father God, I am a member of Your royal race. In Your Son, Jesus Christ, I am a king and a priest unto You. I am Your workmanship, created in Christ Jesus to do the works You have prepared for me to accomplish. With my life, I will  bring honor and glory to You. I will live in such a way that others will be drawn to You, Father, in Jesus' precious name. I will make a difference in the quality of life for multitudes because I have been infused with Your creativity and ingenuity. Hallelujah!

Ephesians 2:10; Revelation 1:6

———————— CONFESSION ————————

God's creativity and ingenuity in me are enhanced through the empowering of the Holy Spirit!

Father, thank You for Your protection. Because I dwell in Your presence and You make Your home in my heart, I abide under Your protection. Your angels have been dispersed to keep charge over me in all of my ways. No evil shall come near me, and plagues are off limits to me because of Your protection. I have nothing to fear, for You have given me all authority over the power of the devil, and You said, Lord Jesus, that nothing would harm me. Hallelujah!

Psalm 91; Luke 10:19

————— CONFESSION —————

I trust in the Lord, Who is my rock, my fortress,
my deliverer and my strength! (Ps. 18:2,3.)

Father God, You will help me speak by putting words in my mouth. Thank You for teaching me what to do in every circumstance. You will show me how to "react" to the words and actions of others.  My words and actions are a reflection of Your character, Father. No one will be able to withstand the wisdom and creativity of Your Spirit, which flows through me like a mighty river, in Jesus' name. Amen.

Exodus 4:12,15,16

———————————— CONFESSION ————————————

God gives me wisdom to speak that no one, not even my enemies, will be able to gainsay or resist! (Luke 21:15.)

Heavenly Father, You are my light and my salvation. Therefore, I shall not fear man nor become entangled in the traditions of men. I throw aside every weight and sin that has tried to ensnare me that I might run the race You have set before me with confidence, victory, efficiency and effectiveness. I want You to be glorified through my life, in Jesus' name. Amen.

Psalm 27:1; Hebrews 12:1; 1 Corinthians 9:24-26

———————————— C O N F E S S I O N ————————————

I'm running after the Lord to receive a crown
of eternal blessedness that will not wither.

Father, I watch over the affairs of my household with Your Word as the standard for my thoughts, words and actions. Because I do not eat of the bread of idleness and I am diligent in my work, I will stand before kings. My household will serve as a model of godliness to others in Jesus' name. Amen.

Proverbs 22:29; Proverbs 31:27

———————— CONFESSION ————————

My primary goal in life is to become
a reflection of the Lord Jesus Christ!

Father God, I will not use the freedom You have so graciously given me as an opportunity to appease my flesh. Instead, I will use it as an avenue to serve the other members of the Body of Christ through the work and ministry to which You have called me. By Your love I will serve. By Your wisdom and discernment I will respond to the needs of others. By Your Spirit, I will know when someone needs an encouraging word, food, clothing, or financial or spiritual help, and I will come to their aid, in Jesus' name. Amen.

Galatians 5:13

———— CONFESSION ————

As a servant of the Lord, I am kind to everyone,
able to teach and not quarrelsome or resentful. (2 Tim. 2:24.)

Heavenly Father, thank You for restoring health to me and healing my wounds. Though my home is not in this world, I am a temporary resident in the world arena. Because Your healing virtue is working in me, I'll not accept the rejection, the bruising, or the piercing of negative words or actions in my mind. I'll not accept symptoms of any kind that would mar the well-being of my physical body. Nothing but the pureness of Your Word will feed my spirit, Lord. In the name of Jesus, I am healed and whole in spirit, body and mind. Amen.

Jeremiah 30:17

——————— CONFESSION ———————

All is well because God is moving behind the scenes for me!

 I will praise You, Lord, as long as I live, giving thanks for Your benefits: forgiveness of all sin; healing of every sickness and disease; redemption from destruction; crowning with loving-kindness and tender mercies; satisfying my mouth with good things; and renewing my youth as an eagle – strong, overcoming and soaring!

Psalm 103:1-5; Psalm 146:2

CONFESSION

I will worship the Lord in the splendor of His holiness. (Ps. 29:2.)

Father God, though my enemies appear to be overwhelming in the natural, I will not be afraid. You are with me, and You will help me. You are faithful, Lord. Just as You have delivered me in the past, You will do it again. I  accept Your strategies so I can run like a champion in this life. I accept Your witty inventions and creative ideas, Lord, that will put me ahead of even the finest of the world's competitors. There is no defeat for me because I am anchored into You, Father, in Jesus' name. Amen.

Deuteronomy 20:1-4

——————— CONFESSION ———————

*No one will be able to stand against me
all the days of my life. (Josh. 1:5.)*

Lord Jesus, You have given me the ability to discern between sheep and wolves. I can identify a person's spirituality by the fruit coming from his or her life. A good person bears good fruit, and a bad person bears bad fruit. I bear good fruit, even in a time of drought. That's because my confidence and trust are in You, Lord. You are a good Father to me, in Jesus' name. Amen.

Jeremiah 17:7,8; Matthew 7:16-20

—————— CONFESSION ——————

Because I remain in the Lord and He remains in me,
I will bear much fruit. (John 15:5.)

Heavenly Father, I will meditate upon Your Word day and night, and I will be an obedient doer of Your Word, so my pathway will be prosperous and successful. Because Your Word dominates my thoughts, words and actions, I will not be seduced or deceived by the works of the devil. I will be strong in You, Lord, and in the power of Your might.

Joshua 1:8; Matthew 24:4,5

———————————— C O N F E S S I O N ————————————

I am building my life upon the Rock of God's Word.

Lord Jesus, You said that what comes out of a person's heart is what makes him [or her] unclean. "From within...come evil thoughts, sexual immorality, theft, murder, adultery, greed, malice, deceit, lewdness, envy, slander, arrogance and folly. All these evils...make a man 'unclean.'" Thank You for cleansing me with Your shed blood, Lord Jesus. You have blotted out and canceled my transgressions. You have no remembrance or record of my sin, because true repentance and a turning from it have taken place in me, in the name of Jesus. Hallelujah!

Isaiah 43:25, AMP; Mark 7:20-23

———————————— CONFESSION ————————————

God has created a pure heart and
a steadfast spirit within me. (Ps. 51:10.)

Lord Jesus, I will not be afraid, but I will stand firm upon the promises of Your Word. You will deliver me from every evil plot and scheme of the enemy. The enemies I face today I shall never see again. Because You are fighting for me, Lord, I will hold my peace and remain at rest, knowing that victory is mine!

Exodus 14:13,14

——————————— C O N F E S S I O N ———————————

I am the apple of God's eye.
Whoever touches me touches Him. (Zech. 2:8.)

 Lord, You are my strength, my rock, my fortress, my deliverer and my shield. My enemies will not triumph over me. Because my ways are pleasing to You, Lord, You make my enemies to be at peace with me. You cause my enemies to flee from me seven ways. You honor me by preparing a table of abundance for me in the presence of my enemies, in Jesus' name. Amen.

Deuteronomy 28:7; Psalm 18; Psalm 23:5; Proverbs 16:7

———————— CONFESSION ————————

I have been given authority to overcome all the power of the enemy. Nothing will harm me or my family. (Luke 10:19.)

Heavenly Father, every day I walk as a sheep among wolves, yet I am not hindered. I am not harmed. I am not deceived. Because Your Spirit makes His home in me, I am wise as a serpent. I am innocent, harmless, guileless and without falsity as a dove. My victory often comes as I allow a meek and quiet spirit to dominate me, Lord Jesus. Thank You for making me courageous, yet discreet. Confident, yet humble. Overcoming, yet not obnoxious. Hallelujah!

Matthew 10:16, AMP; 1 Peter 3:4

———————————— C O N F E S S I O N ————————————

I am filled with godly wisdom, and God's grace
and mercy clothe me. (Luke 2:40.)

Father God, You said in Your Word that greater is He, Jesus Christ, Who is in me, than he, the devil, who is in the world. As a born-again believer, You have called me to the ministry of reconciliation – to bring people into relationship with You, Lord Jesus. You have also called me an ambassador, one who represents You in the earth. In Jesus' name, I will represent You well. Amen.

2 Corinthians 5:18-20; 1 John 4:4

——— CONFESSION ———

I will pull someone from the clutches of hell today!

Heavenly Father, because You have turned my captivity and have done great things for me, my mouth is filled with laughter and my tongue with singing. Joy floods my being, and rejoicing covers my lips! The dark clouds of oppression have been replaced with Your goodness, Father. It is well with me because of Whose I am and Whom I serve, in Jesus' name. Amen.

Job 8:21; Psalm 126; Zechariah 9:17

———————————— C O N F E S S I O N ————————————

The cheerfulness of my heart is as medicine
to my spirit, body and mind. (Prov. 17:22.)

Heavenly Father, You said in Your Word that You would forgive me as I forgive and release others. Help me to be quick to forgive others as well as myself. I am daily washed in the water of Your Word. I am also washing others with Your Word, Lord, framing their lives with what You say about them. As I help others to grow spiritually, it enhances my own growth in Jesus' name. Amen.

Matthew 6:12-15; Mark 11:25,26; John 20:23

———— C O N F E S S I O N ————

I have great peace because I love God's laws. Nothing shall offend me or cause me to stumble. (Ps. 119:165, AMP).

My life is complete in You, Lord Jesus. That means every answer, every need, every solution I have need of is available in You! You are Jehovah-Rapha, my Healer. Jehovah-Nissi, my Banner of Victory. Jehovah-Jireh, my Provider. Jehovah-M'Kaddesh, my Sanctifier. Jehovah-Shalom, my Peace and Security. Jehovah-Rohi, my Shepherd. Jehovah-Tsidkenu, my Righteousness. And Jehovah-Shammah, my ever-present Friend. I am complete in You, Lord Jesus. Amen.

Colossians 2:10

CONFESSION

With the Holy Spirit as my Guide, I am able
to walk blameless before God! (Gen. 17:1.)

Father, I obey Your voice and walk in all the ways You have commanded in Jesus' name. You are my Father, and I am Your child. It is well with me — spiritually, mentally, physically, socially, emotionally and financially. Thank You for guiding me in my walk with You, Father, so I'll do the most damage to Satan's kingdom and do the most good to Your Kingdom every day, in Jesus' name. Amen.

Psalm 37:23; Jeremiah 7:23; Luke 10:19;

———————— CONFESSION ————————

*I am wise in that which is good
and simple concerning evil. (Rom. 16:19.)*

Father, as I speak words which are in alignment with Your Word, the mountains of adversity which have come at me are disheveled and dissolved. This includes the mountains in my personal life, in business, in ministry, or in relationships. They have no choice but to go from me because of the power and authority in Your name, Lord Jesus. The victories You have given me, Father, far outweigh the adversities that have tried to devour me. I am a winner, and I am an overcomer in Jesus' name. Amen.

Mark 11:22,23

CONFESSION

I'll not be weakened by adversity. Instead, I will be strengthened, because Jesus Christ has already redeemed me from every work of the devil!

Father, You have created me to live this life as a leader – above and not beneath. With Your help, I will be the head and not the tail. Always at the top! Never at the bottom! Filled with counsel and might, not with doubt, despair and defeat. In the name of Jesus, I will complete every assignment You give me, Lord, because I am infused with Your ability! Hallelujah!

Deuteronomy 28:13

─────────── CONFESSION ───────────

I press toward the mark for the prize of the high calling of God in Christ Jesus (Phil. 3:14).

Heavenly Father, I cast the whole of my care – all anxieties, worries and concerns – upon You once and for all. I know You love me and care for me. I make all my requests known to You with thanksgiving. Because I know You hear  me, I believe Your "best" answers are on the way the moment I pray, in Jesus' name. Amen.

Philippians 4:6; 1 Peter 5:7, AMP

——————— C O N F E S S I O N ———————

I give thanks to the Lord for His goodness. (Ps. 136:1.)

Thank You, Lord, that You will never leave me nor forsake me. You are always with me through the Holy Spirit Who is my Comforter, Counselor, Helper, Advocate, Intercessor, Strengthener, Teacher and Guide. I will not fear or be dismayed, Father, for You hold me up with Your victorious right hand in Jesus' name. Amen.

Isaiah 41:10, AMP; John 15:26, AMP; Hebrews 13:5

———————— C O N F E S S I O N ————————

I will not be afraid, for God is my Friend and Helper!

Father God, I have made a decision that as for me and my household, we will serve You. I lay down the gods of this world, some of which have had such a grip on me that my priorities have been out of order. Help me to rearrange my priorities, Lord Jesus, so recreation, work, sports, food, money, clothes, pleasure and anything else that I have put ahead of You be brought into a proper balance. Amen.

Joshua 24:15

CONFESSION

There is no god like my God — in heaven or on earth!
He is worthy of all praise. (2 Chron. 6:14.)

Thank You, Father, for redeeming my life from destruction with the awesome price of the blood of Your Son. You saw value in me to pay such a price for me. Jesus' precious blood paid the price for the divine destiny You placed in me, Father, which I will live out to the full. You loved me to weave within me such a purpose. Thank You for Your unconditional love. Help me to love others with Your love, in Jesus' name. Amen.

Mark 12:30,31; John 3:16; 1 John 4:7,8

———————— C O N F E S S I O N ————————

The God-kind of love dominates me
and believes the best of every person. (1 Cor. 13:7.)

Father, thank You for the integrity of Your Word. As Jeremiah said, Your Word is like a fire. It burns up sin and dismantles the activities of the devil. It is like a hammer that breaks rock in pieces. Nothing can withstand Your Word, Father, for it is truth, life and health. I am applying Your Word to every circumstance that confronts me. Your Word will cause me to triumph in every situation, hurdle, or trial in Jesus' name. Amen.

Jeremiah 23:29

—————————— CONFESSION ——————————

The effects of God's Word in my life will
always bring success, triumph and gladness of heart!

Father God, I acknowledge You as God in heaven above and on earth below. There is no other God but You! I keep your decrees and commands. Obedience is the key for everything to go well with me and my children. I will live long in the land – the home, the marriage, the relationships, the ministry, the workplace – You have given me, Lord. My life is productive for Your Kingdom, in Jesus' name. Amen.

Deuteronomy 4:39,40

———————— CONFESSION ————————

It is well with me and my seed,
for I keep God's commandments. (Deut. 5:29.)

Father, thank You for making me fruitful in spite of persecution, just as You did Joseph. Because I abide in You and You abide in me, Lord, I will bear fruit that will bring honor and glory to You. I am quick to forgive and release those who offend, Lord, so there is no blockage to fruit-bearing in my life.

Genesis 41:51,52; Matthew 6:12,14,15; John 15:1-8; Matthew 6:12,14,15

――――――――――― CONFESSION ―――――――――――

*All nations call me happy and blessed,
for my life is a land of delight. (Mal. 3:12.)*

Lord Jesus, You are the first love of my life. Nothing – no activity, work, or relationship – has meaning without You at the center of it. My heart's desire is to give others purpose and meaning for life that can only be found in You. I want to impart the flames of hope into them – the kind You have given me, Father. Because of putting You first, heaven's blessings are overtaking me, in Jesus' name. Amen.

Psalm 69:6; Matthew 6:33

—————————————— C O N F E S S I O N ——————————————

My hope and expectation are in the Lord. (Ps. 39:7.)

Heavenly Father, I am singing a new song to You to welcome the new life You have prepared for me. Though I cannot change anything that was good or bad in the past, I can be a blessing to someone today in Jesus' name. I release  the past so I am free to accept the new. I will not judge the new by the patterns of the old. Instead, I accept the complete new thing on its own merits — the friendships, relationships, assignments, responsibilities and blessings. Thank You, Lord Jesus, for Your goodness to me! Amen.

Isaiah 42:9,10, AMP; Isaiah 43:18,19

———— C O N F E S S I O N ————

The earth is full of God's unfailing love. (Ps. 33:5.)

Father, in Jesus' name there is no bondage this side of Heaven that can get a grip on me! You have set me free with Your outstretched arm. Thank You for redeeming me. Thank You for liberating me from the works of the devil. Thank You for walking with me each day. Thank You for keeping me free through the power of the Holy Spirit. Amen.

Exodus 6:6,7; Leviticus 26:12,13

—————— CONFESSION ——————

Words and actions that are not of God
cannot prevail against me! The enemy will be
exposed and brought to defeat in my behalf!

Father, thank You for restoring the years the devil has stolen from my life. I shall have plenty to eat – spiritually as well as physically. I praise You, Lord, that no more will I or any of Your children be ashamed, for You alone are the Lord. Wondrous are Your works in the midst of me!

Joel 2:25,27

———————— CONFESSION ————————

Because God has arisen in my life,
my enemies are scattered and my foes
flee from me! (Ps. 68:1.)

Heavenly Father, thank You for showing Yourself strong in my behalf. You cause divine connections and divine appointments which benefit me to spring forth. You cause me to be a wise steward of the finances You place in my hand by leading me to sales and the best buys. You cause me to hear supernatural guidelines that will put me ahead of worldly competition. You are doing great things for me in the name of Jesus. Amen.

2 Chronicles 16:9; Psalm 126:2,3

— CONFESSION —

I have replaced the lower life in the natural
for the higher life of the Spirit! (Matt. 10:39.)

Father, I have fixed my eyes upon You as the author and perfecter of my faith. I will run the race of this life with excellence as my goal. Second best has no place in me. I will run with the intent of achieving first-class in every area of life. Remove from me anything that encumbers and binds. In the name of Jesus, I am stepping into Your yoke which is easy, and I am accepting Your burden which is light. Amen.

Matthew 11:28-30; Hebrews 12:1,2

———————————— CONFESSION ————————————

With God's help, I will do mighty acts of valor! (Ps. 108:13.)

Father, in Jesus' name, every place the sole of my foot treads is mine! Spiritually and naturally, I possess the land where You direct me to be, Father. No one can take it from me. It's a land of milk and honey – of untold blessings! Obedience to Your commands and confession of Your Word are keys to possession, in Jesus' mighty name. Amen.

Deuteronomy 1:8;6:18; 8:1; 11:8,9; Joshua 1:3

CONFESSION

Because I do that which is right and good
in God's sight, it is well with me.

Heavenly Father, everything in Your Word points to the fact that it is Your plan to increase me in every area of my life. In prosperity as well as in responsibility and in promotions to positions of leadership. In the name of Jesus, I will be careful never to set my heart upon riches or authority. My focus will remain upon You, Lord, and how I can best serve You by serving others well! Hallelujah!

Psalm 62:10

— C O N F E S S I O N —

The Lord is the source of all of my increase!

Father, Solomon said, "I am my beloved's, and my beloved is mine." I am Your beloved, Father, and You are mine in the name of Jesus. As a husband protects and cares for his wife, so You protect and care for me. I am Your servant, following Your example of servanthood. Mold me into Your image that I may serve others with a pure heart. Enable me by Your Spirit to make decisions and perform feats that will turn the world right-side up, in Jesus' name. Amen.

Song of Solomon 6:3

———————————— CONFESSION ————————————

Because I am great in God's Kingdom,
I am a servant to others. (Matt.20:27.)

Cleanse me, Lord, from all impurities and put a new heart and a new spirit within me. Remove my heart of stone and give me a heart of flesh that will be sensitive and compassionate to the needs of others. In Jesus' name, help me to see others as You see them and to hear and answer their cries just as You would.

Ezekiel 36:25-28

―――――――――― CONFESSION ――――――――――

*I have a servant's heart, and I am following the example
of the greatest servant Who ever lived, Jesus Christ!*

Father, some situations which initially appear to offer rejection are ultimately for my protection. Help me to see the difference and trust You for what I do not understand. Help me to see and hear with spiritual eyes and ears so I'll not be deceived. Your Word says that what the enemy meant for harm, You will turn for my good, Father. Thank You for working all things together for my good in Jesus' name. Amen.

Genesis 50:20; Romans 8:28

—————————— CONFESSION ——————————

I will trust in the Lord at all times,
for His ways are perfect. His name is a strong tower,
and in Him I am safe. (Ps. 62:8; Prov. 18:10.)

Your Kingdom, Father, is composed of righteousness, peace and joy in the Holy Spirit. Because You rule my life, my attitudes, words and actions are dominated by the characteristics of Your quality of life. I am daily influencing others with Your life. You are increasing in me, Lord, and I am decreasing. You are increasing and abounding in the earth, overtaking the devil's works. I am part of this victorious transition! Hallelujah!

Romans 14:17

———————————— CONFESSION ————————————

I have been created to reign on this earth! (Rev. 5:10.)

Lord Jesus, like Paul, I will pray with my spirit, and I will pray with my mind. I will sing with my spirit, and I will sing with my understanding. Thank You, Father, for giving me interpretation by the Holy Spirit of that which I speak unto You in another tongue. Through the prophet Isaiah, You said You would speak to me through another tongue. You also said that praying in the Spirit would cause me to be rested and refreshed. Father, I receive Your rest and refreshing so I can be even more productive for You, in the name of Jesus. Amen.

Isaiah 28:11,12; 1 Corinthians 14:13-15

CONFESSION

I am built up and strengthened as I pray in the Spirit. (Jude 20.)

Father, because I am in covenant with You, Your joy and peace lead me. The mountains and the hills break forth into singing before me. The trees of the field clap their hands in rejoicing as I walk out Your plans, in spite of  natural opposition. All Heaven rejoices as I walk in obedience to You. All Heaven also rejoices as I win every battle in this life, in Jesus' name. Amen.

Isaiah 55:12

———————————— C O N F E S S I O N ————————————

My daily walk with the Lord is adventuresome and delightful!

 Heavenly Father, thank You for directing and establishing my steps. Each day I literally step into the footsteps You have walked before me because of the leading of the Holy Spirit. My steps are anointed with divine wisdom. They are anointed with love and truth. With discretion, power and authority. With championship qualities that are being developed in me. I am a champion in the making in Jesus' name. Amen.

Psalm 37:23; Proverbs 4:11,12,18

C O N F E S S I O N

Champions are bred, fed and cleansed with the living water of God's Word! I am a champion for Christ!

Heavenly Father, as I partake of the physical food set before me which You have blessed, new life and vitality flood my spirit, body and soul. Symptoms of sickness and disease have no choice but to leave me. Mental oppression  that opposes soundness of mind has to leave me. Spiritual weakness and inferiority can't reside in me. You have created me to be superior and blessed, Father. All is well with me in every area of my life, in the name of Jesus! Amen.

Exodus 23:25; Isaiah 53:5

———————————— CONFESSION ————————————

Because my soul is prospering in God's Word,
my body is healed and whole. (3 John 2.)

Father God, I love Your Word. It is as fresh and alive today as the day it was written. It dwells in me richly, enabling me to teach and admonish others with Your wisdom. It enables me to connect others to You, Lord Jesus, because You are Wisdom! You will keep me from being moved off course with false doctrines of the devil and the flippant ideas of man. Your counsel stands sure, and it comes forth in psalms, hymns and spiritual songs. Thank You for helping me to grow up spiritually in You, Lord Jesus, and to help others grow, too! Amen.

Colossians 3:16

--- CONFESSION ---

Daily, I am growing up spiritually in the wisdom of the Lord, for Wisdom lives within me through the Holy Spirit!

Heavenly Father, Joel 3:10 contains one of Your patterns for living in victory. You said, "Let the weak say, I am strong [a warrior]!" (AMP). Another translation of this verse says, "Let the weak say, 'I am a mighty man'" (NAS). I am strong. I am healthy. I have Your wisdom, Lord. Your anointing flows in me, causing the work of my hands to be absolutely outstanding! There is no life of adventure like that found in You, in the name of Jesus. Amen.

Joel 3:10 (AMP, NAS)

——————————— C O N F E S S I O N ———————————

I can do everything God asks me to do
with the help of Christ. (Phil. 4:13, TLB.)

Father God, just as You brought Joseph hastily out of the dungeon and promoted him from prison to second in command in a single day, my promotion from You is on its way. It will cause the persecution and affliction I have experienced for standing for Your truth to seem insignificant. You are the Deliverer out of all affliction, Lord, and You are able to use it as a springboard for greatness!

Genesis 41:14,39-43; Psalm 34:19; Psalm 75:6,7

—————————— C O N F E S S I O N ——————————

Though my beginning was small, my ending shall be prosperous and greatly increased. (Job 8:7.)

Lord Jesus, You commanded that I love others as You have loved me. You have not asked me to criticize or judge but to love. You have not asked me to manipulate relationships for personal gain, but just to love with Your  love. You are love, Lord Jesus, and I am accepted and loved by You. You are reconstructing me so I can love others without partiality. I'll be quick to identify and encourage the good in others because of Your love in me, Lord. Amen.

John 13:34,35

———— CONFESSION ————

My life is a live demonstration of the love of God as I love others as He would love them. (1 John 4:7.)

Father God, I pray for the one I love so dearly today, my mate.* You joined us together, and we are committed to one another with all of our hearts. In You, Lord Jesus, we have become one flesh. We will not tolerate strife or disharmony in our hearts, in our marriage, or in our home. Daily, we verbally encourage the good in each other, and silently we pray for one another's weak areas. Our relationship is seasoned with a daily time of prayer together. A spirit of laughter and joy dominates us. We are becoming more in love with each other every day, in Jesus' name. Amen.

Deuteronomy 32:30; Matthew 19:6; Ephesians 5:31

———————— CONFESSION ————————

Divorce is not an option in my marriage. I am committed to my mate, because I accepted my covenant vows of marriage for keeps!
* (If you are not married, pray for someone else's marriage.)

Heavenly Father, thank You for the avenues You have prepared through which divine guidance can flow into my life. Your Word, the prompting of the Holy Spirit and Your still, small voice guide me. The anointed teaching and preaching of Your servants offer guidance. I will never veer off of the course You have set for me, because my ears and eyes are spiritually alert, in the name of Jesus. Amen.

1 Kings 19:12; John 16:13; Acts 2:17,18

——————————————— CONFESSION ———————————————

Because I acknowledge the Lord, He directs my path
with intimate detail. (Prov. 3:6.)

Father God, I have made a decision to be willing and obedient to Your commands. Willingness and obedience set the stage for great miracles. I shall eat the good of the land – in physical as well as spiritual food! In wisdom and understanding. In knowledge and discernment. In relationships. In wholeness and soundness. In open doors to the opportunities You want me to accept, Lord. In the name of Jesus, I am prospering in every area of life! Thank You, Lord!

Isaiah 1:19

———— CONFESSION ————

I will obey God's voice and serve Him. (Josh. 24:24.)

Thank You, Father, for the wonderful benefits You have provided for me through Jesus' completed work at Calvary: Forgiveness, healing, redemption and crowning me with loving-kindness and tender mercies. I am strong and overcoming in You, Lord Jesus. Because I am infused with Your strength and ability, I soar through my daily responsibilities as an eagle in Jesus' name. Amen.

Psalm 103:1-6

———————————— C O N F E S S I O N ————————————

Each day of my life, the Lord loads me
with His benefits. (Ps. 68:19.)

Heavenly Father, You said that life is in the blood. When I was born again, I received a new bloodline – a transfusion of pure blood from You replacing my old bloodline that was contaminated with sin and generational curses. An exchange took place that brought me into Your family, Lord. It cost You everything – the death, burial, resurrection and ascension of Your Son. It costs me nothing but genuine repentance. Thank You for this glorious exchange in the name of Jesus. Amen.

Leviticus 17:11; 1 John 1:7

———————— CONFESSION ————————

*I am purified from all unrighteousness through acceptance
of the shed blood of Jesus Christ. (1 John 1:9.)*

Lord Jesus, You have begun a good work in me. Thank You for carrying it on to completion. I yield myself to You anew this day as a piece of clay to be molded as You will. I yield myself to Your carving and shaping as the Great Carpenter! Thank You for remaking me and for perfecting everything that concerns me in the name of Jesus. Amen.

Psalm 138:8; Philippians 1:6

———————— CONFESSION ————————

The Word of God equips me for every good work. (2 Tim. 3:17.)

Father God, I have put off the life of my old nature – that which is contrary to Your nature. I have literally disowned the characteristics of a selfish life. In You I have been recreated in righteousness and true holiness. I am daily being clothed in more of Your nature and attributes, Lord Jesus. I am so confident in Your ability in me that I am able to perform at the highest level of excellence, in Jesus' name. Amen.

Ephesians 4:22-24

—————————— C O N F E S S I O N ——————————

With every breath, I praise and
worship the living God! (Ps. 150:6.)

Father God, You multiplied the handful of flour and the little jug of oil in the widow woman's hand. The key to multiplication in her life was that she preferred the prophet Elijah before herself and her son with the little sustenance she had. She proved Your principles of multiplication to be true. Help me to prefer others before myself. In Jesus' name, I will step into the rhythm of giving, knowing that my own needs will be abundantly met in the process.

1 Kings 17:7-16

—————————————— CONFESSION ——————————————

As I give, it is given unto me — good measure, pressed down, shaken together and running over! With the same measure I give, it is measured back to me. (Luke 6:38.)

Father, Your Word is life and health and healing to me. I commit a portion of each day to the study and meditation of Your Word. By a quality choice I have made and with the Holy Spirit's help, I am free of the three primary things that choke the effectiveness of Your Word: the cares of this life, the deceitfulness of riches and the desire for "things." In the name of Jesus, Your Word washes the contamination of the world from me and reproduces in me a hundred-fold return! Hallelujah!

Proverbs 4:20-22; Mark 4:13-20

———— CONFESSION ————

I have cast the cares of this life upon the Lord, for He cares for me and provides for me abundantly. (1 Pet. 5:7.)

Heavenly Father, You said in Your Word that my enemies will not triumph over me. Those who transgress against me without a cause will be brought down. Show me Your way, Lord, and lead me in Your truth. Thank You for patience to "walk out" some of the trials brought about by the work of the devil. As I remain steadfast in You, Lord Jesus, my end will be success and I'll not even smell of the smoke from the fiery trials! You said the end of my enemies would be disgrace and shame, in Jesus' name. Amen.

Psalm 25:2-5

———— CONFESSION ————

The integrity and uprightness
of the Lord preserve me. (Ps. 25:21.)

Father God, You are the delight of my life. I will ride upon the high places of the earth, and I will eat of the heritage of Jacob. That's Your plan and promise for me! I cannot comprehend all the wonderful things You have prepared for me, just because I love You, reverence You, obey You and am thankful to You for Your goodness! What a mighty God You are, in Jesus' name. Amen.

Isaiah 58:14; 1 Corinthians 2:9

——————— C O N F E S S I O N ———————

*God will never be outdone! He is working
behind the scenes today on my behalf!*

Heavenly Father, thank You for the rest You have provided for me. I am seeking Your face to know how to pray more effectively and to work more diligently, yet maintain the qualities of rest and peace in my life. I receive Your promise of a secure home – an undisturbed place of rest. The fruit of Your righteousness in me is quietness and confidence forever, in the name of Jesus. Amen.

Isaiah 32:17,18; Hebrews 4:9-11

——————— CONFESSION ———————

God's presence is with me,
and He gives me rest. (Ex. 33:14.)

Father, because I know the voice of the Good Shepherd, I'll not follow the voice of a stranger. Your voice, Lord, always agrees with Your Word, for You and Your Word are one and the same. Because Your Word is truth, it will reveal the false and the counterfeit. Because it is eternal, it will change the temporary. Because it is light, it will repel the darkness. Because it is life, it will swallow up death! Hallelujah!

John 10:4,5,27

--- CONFESSION ---

I am led by the voice of the Good Shepherd.
The voice of a stranger I'll not follow.

Lord Jesus, You are my light and my salvation. I shall not fear. You are my All-Sufficiency, my Redeemer, Provider, Sanctifier, Protector, Healer and Victor! You are El Shaddai. That means You are more than enough for every challenge I am facing, for every decision I must make, for the questions I need answered, for the adjustments I need to make. You are everything to me, Lord Jesus! On You and You alone, I lean, rely and trust!

Psalm 27:1

CONFESSION

My refuge and counsel are in the Lord. (Ps. 34:8.)

Father, thank You for divinely ordering my days and filling them with divine connections, relationships and assignments. Thank You for filling my life with Your grace, mercy and truth. I want people's lives to be changed because of my lifestyle. Because I am accountable to You, Lord, I want my spiritual report card to bring highest honor to You, in Jesus' name. Amen.

Romans 14:11,12

CONFESSION

Because I guard my ways and my words,
my entire life is divinely guarded. (Prov. 16:17.)

Father God, Your Spirit showed up in the fiery furnace with Shadrach, Meshach and Abednego as the Fourth Man! You kept them from being harmed or burned. Yet those who had a role in throwing them into the furnace died from the  intense heat. You confounded the rules of man! Thank You for being the Fourth Man in my life, Lord Jesus, the One Who destroys Satan's plots and wicked schemes with the burning fire of Your breath! Hallelujah!

Daniel 3:19-30

CONFESSION

Promotion is mine for refusing to bow to man's traditions or to other gods, just as it was with the three Hebrew boys. (Dan. 3:28,30.)

 Heavenly Father, You loved me so much that You gave Your very best to save me. You sent Your only Son to purchase me back from the realm of darkness and bring me into the light of Your love. You didn't send Jesus to condemn me. You sent Him to give me an abundant, adventuresome life. Because of Your love for me, Father, it is my aim to owe nothing to anyone but Your kind of love — a love that is revealed in kind words and actions. Amen.

John 3:16,17; Romans 13:8

—————————— CONFESSION ——————————

I have been purchased so I can take the Good News of Jesus Christ into the marketplace, business, ministry, home, neighborhoods and to the ends of the earth!

Heavenly Father, thank You for my pastor and my church family. You said to pray for those in authority over me, which includes my pastor. You also said not to neglect to assemble together with other believers regularly. In the name of Jesus, I ask that a Spirit of wisdom and under-  standing, counsel and might, knowledge and reverential and obedient fear of the Lord rest upon my pastor as well as the Body of Believers of which I am a part. Protect and bless each one, Lord, spiritually, mentally, physically, emotionally and financially, in Jesus' name. Amen.

Isaiah 11:2, AMP; 1 Timothy 2:1-4,8; Hebrews 10:25

─────────── CONFESSION ───────────

My pastor feeds, guides and shields me. My brothers and sisters in God's family encourage, admonish, exhort and edify me, building me up in the Lord. (Ps. 23:1; 1 Thess. 5:11, AMP.)

Heavenly Father, I look to You for promotion, for Your Word says that You are the One Who brings down and the One Who exalts. You also said that my heart attitude should be that of humility for You to exalt me. My goal isn't to get the best for myself, but to be the best for You, Lord. I want Your promotion rather than the promotion of man so I can prosper in that which You have called me to do, in Jesus' name. Amen.

Psalm 75:6,7; Luke 14:11; Luke 18:14

———— CONFESSION ————

*A humble attitude sets the stage
for promotion and honor. (Prov. 15:33.)*

Lord Jesus, wholesome, uplifting talk comes out of my mouth to edify, encourage, exhort and comfort others. You have given me a new nature of kindness, compassion and forgiveness. I am quickened by Your Spirit to speak words that feed life rather than degradation and death into myself and others. In the name of Jesus, my tongue is Holy-Ghost-controlled, pouring out words that build wholesome lives. Amen.

Ephesians 4:29-32; James 3:1-10

——————— CONFESSION ———————

*The wholesome words of my tongue activate
the kind of life I enjoy, just as a rudder
guides a ship to its destination!*

Father, You said that my gift (talents and abilities) will make room for me and bring me before great men. I am asking that the abilities You have placed within me, Lord, be connected to an employment opportunity where I can blossom for You. You said You would supply all of my needs. One of my needs right now is employment so I can provide for my own household. Thank You for leading me to the business or ministry where You want me, or for giving me information and funds to start a self-employment venture, in the name of Jesus. Amen.

Proverbs 18:16; Philippians 4:19; 2 Thessalonians 3:10; 1 Timothy 5:8

—————————— CONFESSION ——————————

God will open the doors of opportunity for employment where He wants me to be, and He will shut the doors where I should not be as I lean to the leading of His Spirit. (Rev. 3:7,8.)

Lord Jesus, You are the Bread of Life. The Father sent You from heaven to share Your life with me. I'll never go hungry nor ever be thirsty – spiritually or naturally – because I'm linked up with You. There's nothing in this world that can cause Your Bread to mold or disintegrate in me because I partake of it fresh each day! Glory to God!

John 6:32,33,35,51

─────────── CONFESSION ───────────

*I have received of the Bread of Life, Who has given me
eternal life and abundant benefits in my present life.*

 You are my refuge and fortress, Lord. My hiding place! In You I trust. You have delivered me from the snares of the devil. You have delivered me from his oppression, which includes sickness, disease, plagues, griefs and sorrows. Your Word is my shield and defense. Satan and his works are crushed under my feet! That's because I'm seated in heavenly places with You, Lord Jesus!

Psalm 91:2-4; Acts 10:38; Ephesians 2:6

—————— CONFESSION ——————

The truth of God's Word sets me free
and keeps me free. (John 8:32,36.)

Lord Jesus, my old life and nature, with its wickedness, are dead and gone. I am a new creation in You. Your shed blood has cleansed and prepared me to be useful for every good work for Your Kingdom. I am pursuing faith, love and peace so I can become a vessel of gold and honor to You, Father, in the name of Jesus. Amen.

2 Corinthians 5:17; 2 Timothy 2:19-22

CONFESSION

I have been redeemed with the precious blood of Christ, a Lamb without blemish or defect. (1 Pet. 1:19.)

Heavenly Father, You have prepared my future. As I am led by Your Spirit, I will walk out Your tailor-made plans for my life. I shall refrain my voice from weeping and my eyes from tears, knowing that my work will be rewarded by You, Lord. I am operating in Your ability and Your anointing in Jesus' mighty name. That's why nothing can cause me to turn back from Your goals for me, Lord Jesus! Hallelujah!

Jeremiah 31:16,17

--------- C O N F E S S I O N ---------

In obeying God's Word,
there is great reward for me! (Ps. 19:11.)

Heavenly Father, my spouse is becoming more like You each day. Considerate! Loving! Kind! Courteous! Understanding! Tender! Spiritually alive and alert! He/she esteems me and delights in me. Because he/she is confident of who he/she is in You, Lord Jesus, he/she loves me as he/she loves himself/herself. My mate freely expresses his/her love to me. He/she honors and lifts me up continually. My spouse and I submit to one another. In Jesus' name, God's unconditional love dominates our thoughts, words and actions toward each other. Amen.

Ephesians 5:1,2,25-33, AMP

———————————— CONFESSION ————————————

My marriage is a living demonstration of Christ's love for me.

Father, when Daniel was in training for the king's service, he took an uncompromised stand that he would not defile himself with the king's rich food and wine. Instead, he asked for a diet of vegetables and water, which he and the three Hebrew boys were allowed to substitute for the rich dainties and wine. Daniel and the three Hebrew boys were found to be ten times better in every matter of wisdom and understanding than all the magicians and enchanters in the entire kingdom. I'll not defile my physical body, Lord. I will eat properly, both physically and spiritually, in Jesus' name. Amen.

Daniel 1:8-20

—————————— CONFESSION ——————————

I will not compromise the standards of God's Word which were established as guidelines for a successful, happy life.

Heavenly Father, thank You for provision, protection and divine wisdom for Your missionaries who have laid down their lives to bring Your Gospel to the ends of the earth. Although every person has been called to missions — to tell others of You, Lord Jesus — strengthen those You have called to pioneer Your work. Stir their hearts anew with compassion for the people they are sent to serve. In Jesus' name, I will be a prayer support and a financial support where You direct me. Amen.

Matthew 28:19,20; Mark 16:15

—————————————— C O N F E S S I O N ——————————————

I have answered God's call to service. When He asked,
"Who will go?" I responded, "Send me, Lord." (Isa. 6:8.)

Heavenly Father, I shall decree things as I am led by Your Spirit. They shall be established and in the fullness of time come into manifestation. Light shines upon my ways. Truth fills my heart and mind. Kindness and compassion flow from my tongue. Diligence accompanies my efforts. Divine energy and wholeness flood my body. Clarity, truth and discretion encompass my thoughts, words and actions in Jesus' name. Amen.

Job 22:28

─────────── CONFESSION ───────────

My life is seasoned with God's grace. (Rev. 22:21.)

Heavenly Father, when Solomon was asked what he desired of You, he said, "...a discerning heart to govern your people and to distinguish between right and wrong." Because Solomon didn't ask for life or wealth or the death  of his enemies, You gave him a wise and discerning heart and added riches and honor to his life. Thank You for giving me a wise and discerning heart to exalt Your Kingdom in the earth, Lord. Thank You for helping me to have right motives in everything I do, in Jesus' name. Amen.

1 Kings 3:5-14

———————————— C O N F E S S I O N ————————————

Because the motives of my heart are right in God's sight,
He will lengthen my days upon the earth. (1 Kings 3:14, AMP).

Lord Jesus, Your blood purged me from dead, carnal works and sin. You gave me a new covenant that basically says, all that I am belongs to You, and all that You are belongs to me. All that I have belongs to You, and all that You have belongs to me. Your eternal inheritance is available to me now. Some of its benefits are healing, soundness of mind, wholeness, provision, forgiveness, spiritual vitality and wisdom. Because of what You did for me, I am walking in highest victory in every area of life, in Jesus' name! Hallelujah!

Hebrews 9:14

———————— CONFESSION ————————

I am free of weakness, sickness, poverty and spiritual dullness because I have accepted the benefits of the sacrifice of Jesus' shed blood. (1 Cor. 11:29,30.)

Father God, my eyes are focused upon You. I receive Your light that drives out every work of darkness. My body is strong and healthy because it is filled with Your light. My thoughts are spiritually sound because my mind is filled with Your light. My emotions are stable and strong because they are nourished with the light of Your Word. My spirit is alive and strong because it is linked to the Spirit of light, love and life. There's no room for darkness in me, in Jesus' name. Amen.

Luke 11:34-36; 1 John 1:5-7

———————————— C O N F E S S I O N ————————————

God's Word is a lamp unto my feet
and a light unto my path. (Ps. 119:105.)

Heavenly Father, thank You for doing a work in my heart, which has caused a positive change in my words. My lips speak life rather than death, blessing rather than cursing. My words construct rather than destruct. They exhort rather than derail. They build and strengthen rather than crush and demolish. They produce hope, healing and courage. In Jesus' name, I am a life-giver. Amen.

Job 27:4; Proverbs 18:20,21

―――――――― CONFESSION ――――――――

The major thrust of my life is to become like Jesus Christ of Nazareth in the earth. (1 John 3:2.)

Heavenly Father, You have called me to be a part of the advancement of Your Kingdom in the earth. I'll press through the temporary hindrances and blockages and move forward with the call You have placed upon my life. I will  press through with force to seize Your Kingdom and share it with others, just as I would press through opposition and obstacles to seize a precious prize! I will be violent, not with man, but with the devil and his works, to advance Your Kingdom, Lord, in Jesus' name. Amen.

Matthew 11:12, AMP

———————————— CONFESSION ————————————

I will obey God's commands to go where He wants me to go and to do what He wants me to do! (Josh. 1:16.)

 Heavenly Father, You are pleased with my work and labor of love in helping and ministering to Your people. I will not become lazy or negligent in reaching beyond myself with love and aid to others. Instead, I will imitate those who through faith and patience inherit Your promises. You want me prospered and blessed, Lord, so I can be a blessing to others, in Jesus' name. Amen.

Hebrews 6:10-12

———— C O N F E S S I O N ————

God wants me to experience the manifested
blessing of each of His promises. (2 Cor. 1:20.)

Father, in Jesus' name, it's time for a fresh cultivation of the ground of my heart, for it to be broken up for the planting of new seed. I want the germination of the seed of Your Word to bring greater revelation and understanding of You, Lord. I want to seek You as never before. I want to be pliable in Your hands, Father. Mold me into a vessel of righteousness for Your purposes, at a level I've not known before, in Jesus' name. Amen.

Hosea 10:12

――――――――――― C O N F E S S I O N ―――――――――――

The Holy Spirit is examining me to test my motives and objectives and further purify them in God's sight. (Ps. 26:2.)

Father, my delight is in You! As I have studied and meditated upon Your Word, it has caused me to flourish like a palm tree: Stately! Upright! Useful! Fruitful! Your Word has caused me to be like a cedar in Lebanon: Majestic! Stable! Durable! Incorruptible! Father, everything I touch prospers for Your Kingdom in Jesus' name. Amen.

Psalm 1:1-3; Psalm 92:12-14, AMP

———— C O N F E S S I O N ————

I am filled with spiritual vitality, trust,
love and contentment. (Ps. 92:14.)

Father God, like Paul, I want to be able to say that I have fought a good fight, I have finished the race set before me and I have kept the faith. Success for completing the race comes from continual meditation of the promises of Your Word, then "living out" the guidelines of Your Word. I am meditating on Your Word day and night. So shall my way be prosperous and successful, in Jesus' name. Amen.

Joshua 1:8; 2 Timothy 4:7

———————— C O N F E S S I O N ————————

God's Word is Spirit and life to me. (John 6:63.)

 Heavenly Father, I thank you that no weapon – not one – formed against me shall ever prosper! Whether it's gossip, slander, or any other weapon, it cannot prevail against me because I'm washed in the cleansing and protective blood of Jesus Christ. The weapons formed against me fall to the ground and die before they can manifest against me! I refuse to be pierced with the darts of the enemy. In the name of Jesus, I have peace, righteousness, security and triumph over all opposition. Amen.

Isaiah 54:17, AMP; James 4:7

———————————— CONFESSION ————————————

God is my Vindicator: vengeance belongs to Him. (Rom. 12:19.)

Thank You for planting me, Lord, giving me a safe, peaceful dwelling. I'll not be moved, except by the nudging of Your Spirit. Neither will the children of wickedness harass me anymore. It's a new day for me! I will run with the vision You have placed in my heart, Lord. I will be diligent, faithful and careful to bring glory to Your name in everything I say and do, in Jesus' precious name. Amen.

1 Chronicles 17:9

——————————— CONFESSION ———————————

My path is like the first gleam of dawn, shining ever brighter till the full light of day. (Prov. 4:18.)

Father, You said in Your Word that no one can serve two masters: God and money. One will be hated and the other will be loved. I am devoted to You, Father, in Jesus' name. Money will serve me rather than me serving money! I will accept it as a means of exchange for propagating Your work in the earth. As I serve You first, Lord, You will provide everything I need in great abundance for Kingdom business! Because my priorities are in divine order, You will trust me with unlimited amounts of money, in Jesus' name. Amen.

Matthew 6:24

――――――― CONFESSION ―――――――

God is entrusting me with an unlimited amount
of resources for Kingdom purposes!

Heavenly Father, You knit me together in my mother's womb. I am fearfully and wonderfully made. You ordained my days before I was born. You knew I would be needed for  such a time as this in the earth. I will fulfill the role You have assigned to me to cause Your Kingdom to dominate the earth. I will help destroy the works of the devil in people's lives. I will bring the Good News of You, Lord Jesus, to as many people as possible – all over the earth!

Esther 4:14; Psalm 139:13-16; 1 John 3:8

CONFESSION

*The Lord knew me and approved of me
even before I was born! (Jer. 1:5, AMP.)*

Father God, in Jesus' name, thank You for filling the hearts and mouths of those in government positions of authority with Your righteousness and justice — from the mayors to the City Council; the leadership of local and state court systems; state governors and their staffs; Congressmen and Supreme Court Justices; the Vice-President and the President. Help them to lead the people of this nation with Your truth! Protect them, in Jesus' name. Amen.

Proverbs 16:12,13, AMP; 1 Timothy 2:1-4

———— CONFESSION ————

*I believe and confess that our President and those in authority
in our government are sensitive to God's wisdom and guidance.*

Lord Jesus, thank You for replacing weariness and discouragement with Your strength, power and fresh hope. As I worship You, Lord, and fellowship in Your presence, I am strengthened. Your strength causes me to soar like an eagle through my daily responsibilities. I will run and not grow weary. I will walk and not faint. In Jesus' name, I will rise up and let Your anointing run full course through my being, Father. I'll hear of new inventions and discoveries in the secret place with You that will be a great blessing to all mankind. Glory to God!

Isaiah 40:28-31

─────────────── C O N F E S S I O N ───────────────

I will sing to the Lord a new song for the glorious things
He has done and is yet doing in me! (Isa. 12:5.)

Father, I want You to be magnified through my life. With godly words and actions and unfailing courage, You will be exalted. With kindness and compassion, Your character will be exemplified. With boldness and authority, yet with ultimate caring, Your nature will be revealed through my life. Praise and glory belong to You as I step into the role ordained for me — to be a reflection of You, Lord Jesus! Amen.

Philippians 1:20

—————————— CONFESSION ——————————

As a servant of the Lord, I continually give praise, worship, honor and thanksgiving to Him. (Ps. 134:1.)

Father God, no harm, disaster, tragedy, or calamity will come to me, for You are my habitation in the name of Jesus. You have commanded Your angels to guard and keep me in all of my ways. The devil has no place in me, for I have shut and sealed off doors that were open because of anger, unforgiveness, bitterness, envy and strife. He is under my feet. Because my love is set upon You, Lord, You protect, deliver and honor me. Hallelujah!

Psalm 91:10-15; Ephesians 4:26,27; James 3:14-16

———————— CONFESSION ————————

Goodness, mercy and unfailing love follow me
all the days of my life. (Ps. 23:6.)

Father, You said in Your Word, "A happy heart is a good medicine and a cheerful mind works healing, but a broken spirit dries the bones." It is a decision to reject the world's medicine of sorrow, brokenness, division and strife, and take generous doses of happy-heart and cheerful-mind medication every day! The joy in serving You, Lord, is my strength. The privilege of meditating in Your Word is the love of my life, in Jesus' name. Amen.

Nehemiah 8:10; Proverbs 17:22

——————————— C O N F E S S I O N ———————————

My cup of joy overflows! (John 15:11, TLB.)

Father God, You see me so valuable and precious that You have engraved a picture of me on the palms of each of Your hands. Your thoughts of me outnumber the grains of sand on the seashore. Regardless of the struggles and failures of my past, You see me as an important, irreplaceable part of the entire Body of Christ and I will contribute to Your Kingdom through my life, Lord. Thank You for loving me with an unconditional love, Father, in Jesus' name. Amen.

Psalm 139:17,18; Isaiah 49:16

CONFESSION

With God's help, I will perform to the maximum potential in me every day — at home, in my marriage or other relationships, at work, school, or wherever I am.

Father God, You said in your Word that though we ask of You in prayer, we will not receive when our motives are evil and selfish. Prayer is not answered if the goal of what we ask is sensual pleasure. Expand my vision beyond "us four and no more," Lord. Remove my stony heart and replace it with a heart of compassion and caring. Replace my selfishness with selflessness, in Jesus' name. Amen.

Ezekiel 36:26; James 4:3

———————— CONFESSION ————————

Because I am a godly leader at the top of God's ranks, I am a servant and I serve others with His love. (Matt. 20:26,27, TLB.)

Heavenly Father, I repent of any thoughts, words, or actions that have been unlike You. Cleanse me with Your blood and Your Spirit. Renew and transform me as I daily feed upon Your Word. Thank You for sending a refreshing to my spirit, body and mind as I spend time in Your presence. Sin, guilt, fear, inferiority and condemnation are swallowed up when genuine repentance is released. In You, Lord Jesus, today is a new day for me!

Acts 3:19; Romans 12:2

———— CONFESSION ————

I am anointed with fresh oil from the Holy Spirit. (Ps. 92:10.)

Father God, You sent Your Son Jesus Christ that I might have life and have it to the full. Satan's nature is to steal, kill and destroy. Neither Satan's nature nor Your nature, Lord Jesus, will ever change. I receive Your abundant life this day, Lord. I accept it in overflowing proportions. Then as I am blessed, I can be a blessing to others to the ends of the earth, in Jesus' name. Amen.

John 10:10

———————————————— CONFESSION ————————————————

I can repay the Lord's goodness to me
by sharing it with others. (Ps. 116:12.)

Heavenly Father, You are I AM to me, just as You were to Moses and the Israelites. Your name is I AM. You are ever-present with me through the indwelling Holy Spirit. You will never fail me. You will never leave me without support. You  will never leave me helpless. And You will never forsake me or relax Your hold on me! Thank You, Father, for Your perfectness and for Your goodness to me! I love You! Amen.

Exodus 3:13-15; Hebrews 13:5, AMP

———————————— CONFESSION ————————————

God is my refuge and strength, an ever-present help
in times of trouble. He is I AM to me! (Ps. 46:1.)

Father, Your Spirit has anointed me to change my world! I will bring good news to the poor. I will bring Your healing to the brokenhearted. I will bring freedom to Satan's captives. I will release those who are in prisons of oppression. I am Your arms extended, Lord, during my reign on this earth. It will be said of me, "It is good that he [she] has been here. He [she] brought the Spirit of Jesus into our midst!"

Isaiah 61:1-3; Luke 4:18

—————————— CONFESSION ——————————

Because I have made it a goal to bring refreshing to others,
I too am refreshed! (Prov. 11:25.)

Father, my aim is for excellence in the quality of life I am pursuing in You! I am following the way of love, because You are love. To live in love is to live in light and life. Your love in me drives out fear, which is the greatest opponent of faith. Faith and love work together and set the stage for me to excel in every arena of life! And I shall excel and bring great glory to You, Father, in the name of Jesus! Amen.

1 Corinthians 14:1; 1 John 4:16-18

———————————— CONFESSION ————————————

I am able to love myself and others
because Christ first loved me! (1 John 4:19.)

Father God, I shall arise to new life this day, just as the paralyzed man, carried by four into Jesus' presence, arose to new life. You commanded this man, "Arise!" Your command to me this day is, "Arise!" I will arise, shaking off the entanglements, hurts, bruises and sins of the past. It's a new day! You will do a new thing in my life, Father, which is no longer my own, but Yours! Hallelujah!

Mark 2:11

C O N F E S S I O N

I will forget the former things and not dwell on the past,
for God is doing a new thing in me. (Isa. 43:19.)

Lord Jesus, deceit was never found in Your mouth. When insults were hurled at You, You did not retaliate. When You suffered, You made no threats. You entrusted Yourself instead to the Father Who judges justly. Help me to be more like You, Lord Jesus. Help me to walk in quietness and confidence through slander or injustice, knowing that the end of me will be good, but the end of the aggressor will not be so good. Iniquity will be revealed and righteousness will prevail in Jesus' name. Amen.

1 Peter 2:22,23

——————————— C O N F E S S I O N ———————————

God's truth, in the end, always prevails over injustice.

Other Books by Word Ministries, Inc.

A Call to Prayer
Prayers That Avail Much — Volume I
Prayers That Avail Much — Volume II
Prayers That Avail Much — Special Edition
Prayers That Avail Much for Mothers
Prayers That Avail Much for Fathers
Prayers That Avail Much for Teens
Prayers That Avail Much for Business Professionals
Prayers That Avail Much — Volume I Spanish Edition
Prayers That Avail Much — Volume 2 Portable Gift Book
The Prayers That Avail Much Daily Calendar

Available from your local bookstore, or by writing:
Harrison House • P.O. Box 35035 • Tulsa, OK 74153